# CRASHED, SMASHED, AND MASHED

## A Trip to Junkyard Heaven

# CRASHED, SMASHED, AND MASHED

## A Trip to Junkyard Heaven

Joyce Slayton Mitchell

PHOTOGRAPHS BY Steven Borns

Tricycle Press
BERKELEY • TORONTO

*For Charlie & Hugh's Mum,*
*Rowena Hammill, and Rex and Arthur's Mom,*
*Carol Scheer,*
*models of entrepreneurial mothers,*
*with love and admiration.*
*—J.S.M.*

*For Caroline Marie Sullivan, niece,*
*who makes stuff out of things.*
*—S.B.*

## Sources and Acknowledgments

We are eternally thankful to the boss of junkyard heaven, Jimmy Gates, who gave us complete access to his recycling business at Gates Salvage Yard, in Hardwick, Vermont. We are especially grateful for the time he took to teach us what we had to know to write and photograph this book. Jimmy's incredible patience while we were on location was extraordinary as we constantly requested, "Cut! Hold that forklift for one more shot," and "Stop the blowtorch while we change film!" realizing that the pace in recycling is on the fast track.

Our special thanks too, to the boss of the counter and office, Helen Rivard Gates, and to her assistant, Lisa Sanville. Helen graciously shared her office with us; she took the time to teach, demonstrate, and verify a great number of recycling facts as well as to line up customers that we could photograph for our book.

It is a pleasure to thank the boss of the yard, Bobby McLane, who enthusiastically got us to the right spot at the right time. We want to thank each of the dismantlers and drivers in the yard who were good sports about working with a camera and notebook in their face: Johnathan Gates, Gary Hall, Rodney Keough, Ed Massey, Joe Rivard, Shawn Tardif, and Scott Young.

We appreciate the quick and thorough responses from Brad P. Slater, Public Relations Manager of Automotive Recyclers Association (ARA), Fairfax, Virginia, and the folks at United Recyclers Group (URG), Denver, Colorado, for their interest in our book and their generous sharing of statistics, video, and brochures describing the automotive recycling process.

Working together with Jimmy Gates and his crew, both photographer and writer found that it was a sad day when we had to finally say good-bye to junkyard heaven.

# "COME PICK UP THIS CAR!"

Crashed and smashed cars arrive in junkyard heaven on a flatbed truck. Many of these cars were smashed because they were going too fast. Some crashed on slippery wet and icy roads. Still others fell apart because they were just plain worn out.

## DRAINING FLUIDS

A forklift picks up the car and places it on the lift where seven fluids are removed: gas from the gas tank, oil from the engine, transmission fluid from the transmission, water from the radiator, antifreeze from the radiator and windshield washer, brake fluid from the master cylinder, and freon from the air conditioner.

antifreeze

# UP ON THE FORKLIFT

Tires are taken off the car when the car is in the air. The tires with a good tread are sold to be used again. The worn-out tires are thrown into a sea of tires until they are sold to be shredded and made into new rubber products. While the car is still up on the forklift, the catalytic converter is dismantled.

# TORCHING METALS

A blowtorch shoots intense heat on a small area to melt and separate metal parts such as the starter, transmission, water pump, and alternator.

# PULLING ENGINES

Good engines and transmissions are unbolted and forklifted out of a car to be used in other cars. Damaged engines and radiators have all their removable metals torched off—cast iron, zinc, lead, aluminum, copper, and steel are sold to be used for new metal products.

before

after

# RECYCLING BATTERIES AND RADIOS

The good batteries and radios are stored on shelves in the office for resale. About a ton of dead batteries—from 50 to 70 batteries depending on their size—are put on a pallet and sold to a recycling center for their lead, acid, and plastic.

# REMOVING SHEET METAL ASSEMBLIES

Sheet metal is the thinnest metal on a car used to make car doors, fenders, trunk lids, hatchbacks, and hoods. Sheet metal is often removed and sold in one piece, called an assembly. A door is an assembly that includes the sheet metal, glass windows, plastic handles, trim, and fabric. The front-end assembly includes the hood, fenders, grill, bumper, lights, and trim.

# RESTING IN JUNKYARD HEAVEN

After fluids are drained and some parts are recycled, the good cars and parts remain in a special resting place in junkyard heaven according to their make, model, and year. Their parts will be sold to garages, mechanics, repair shops, and anybody who needs a part.

# FINDING AND BUYING THE RIGHT PART

```
CAPS FDX
                              * Walk-in *                              1 of 1
    Part: HOD          Model: ESCORT          Year: 1995      Int #: 1363
                                 GATES SALVAGE,INC            List:    272
  # Model  Yr Cond   Int-User Description                 Whsl   Retail St
  1-ESCORT 95 0HR     -BLUE,REAL NICE SHAPE              75.00   100.00
  2-ESCORT 95 0HR     -RED, SMALL DENT IN FRONT          50.00    75.00
  3-ESCORT 92 0HR     -TEAL GREEN,                       75.00   100.00



  _____

  When replacing '91-93 hood with '94-96 front hood seal replacement is required.
  Use Ford #F4CZ16A238A.  '91-94 Tracer fills space, but visually is different.
  ID #s: F0CZ16612A,F3CZ16612A,F4CZ16612A,F5CZ16612A



  Help     Orion    Change    Notes    Apps
  Alt-H    Alt-O    Alt-C     Alt-L    Alt-A
  Enter: (#)Sell/Hold, Part Code, (Q)uit <Q> : █
```

Computers help customers find the right part to fix their car. The person at the counter searches the auto parts database to find the years, makes, and models that can be used for the customer's car and the cost of the part.

# TORCH BUGGY DELIVERS

Sometimes customers walk through the junkyard to find parts. When they find the perfect windshield or fender or tailgate or bumper, the dismantler drives his torch buggy to the car to torch and dismantle the part. Other times customers bring their own toolboxes and pull the part they want by themselves or with the dismantler.

# THE CRASHED ARE MASHED...

After the good parts are removed, many smashed cars are picked up by the forklift and fed to the crusher. The crusher compresses the cars until they are mashed to two feet high.

# ...AND STASHED

Three or four mashed cars are stacked one on top of another into bundles. Two tiers each with 10 or 11 cars in each tier—and a combined weight of about 21 tons—are loaded and chained onto the flatbed trailer ready to leave junkyard heaven.

# THE MONSTER SHREDDING MACHINE

The flatbeds of mashed cars are taken to a recycling shredding center where a monster machine rips four or five flatbeds of mashed cars at a time into fist-sized pieces of metals. Its sifters, blowers, and magnets sort the ripped-up pieces into ferrous and nonferrous metals. At the same time, the fluff is separated out and the massive machine spits out different materials, including plastic, glass, carpet fibers, rubber, and seat foam, from each conveyor belt. These recycled metals and fluff are sold to manufacturing companies all over the world.

# OUT WITH THE MASHED...
## IN WITH THE SMASHED

As soon as one flatbed of mashed cars leaves junkyard heaven, the owner of another smashed car calls...

"Come pick up this car!"

# JUNKYARD TALK AND GLOSSARY

**alternator:** part that keeps battery charged

**antifreeze:** liquid that prevents the water in the radiator and windshield wipers from freezing

**assembly:** one piece of sheet metal that can include glass, plastic, trim, and fabric

**blowtorch:** instrument used with oxygen to melt metals

**brake fluid:** liquid that helps a vehicle stop when brake pedal is pushed

**catalytic converter:** cleans exhaust gasses from a vehicle's engine

**clam truck:** flatbed truck with a claw that picks up and loads vehicles onto the truck

**crusher:** large, heavy machine that flattens vehicles

**database:** collection of information organized for specific purposes

**dismantle:** take something apart

**engine:** power unit that makes a vehicle run

**flatbed truck:** truck with a long body without sides

**fluff:** recycled materials other than metals, such as glass, plastic, seat foam, rubber, upholstery fibers, and carpet

**ferrous materials:** iron parts of vehicles

**freon:** chemical that makes air conditioners and refrigerators cold

**forklift:** machine with two flat prongs used to lift vehicles around the yard

**junkyard heaven:** name used in this book for the facility where crashed and smashed vehicles are dismantled so their parts can be reused or recycled; also called a salvage yard or auto recycling center

**lift:** raised platform that holds vehicle

**make:** manufacturer's brand name, like Ford

**master cylinder:** canister that holds brake fluid

**model:** body style of vehicle, like Ranger or Explorer

**nonferrous materials:** nonmagnetic metals, such as aluminum, copper, stainless steel, and brass

**pallet:** four-foot square wooden platform that holds materials for storage and transport

**pole-barn:** open-sided building, with roof held up by interspersed wooden poles

**pull:** remove a part, as in "pull a taillight," "pull a front-end assembly"

**radiator:** cooling system of a vehicle, copper honeycomb design

**tailgate:** end flap on the back of pick-up

**scrap metal:** metal in vehicles that can be reused or recycled

**sheet metal:** flat pieces of metal used on doors, fenders, and hoods

**shredder:** monster machine that includes the mill, rotor, conveyor belts, magnets, and blowers

**skidsteer:** small forklift used to move a pallet of dead batteries

**starter:** turns over motor to start engine

**tread:** layers of rubber on a tire

**torch buggy:** vehicle used in junkyard heaven to carry the blowtorch and oxygen tank to the dismantling site

**transmission:** gear box that transmits engine power to the wheels

**transmission fluid:** liquid that lubricates the gears to make a vehicle run smoothly

**trim:** decorative molding of chrome, plastic, or rubber

**unbolt:** take off the nuts and bolts that hold some vehicle parts in place

**water pump:** pumps coolant through engine and radiator

# RECYCLING FACTS

* Automobile recycling centers and salvage yards are the largest volume recyclers of natural resources in the world.

* Using smashed and mashed cars for their parts and raw materials is big business in the automobile industry. Twelve million cars are reclaimed each year in the United States and Canada.

* These 12 million vehicles save the following raw materials and resources each year:

   85 million barrels of oil
   6 million tires
   2 million tons of cast iron
   7 million tons of steel
   1/2 million ton of aluminum
   1 million pounds of freon

* Salvage yards like junkyard heaven provide car owners with used parts and also save our earth from dangerous pollution. If not drained from smashed and crashed cars, fluids would pollute our earth by seeping into the ground, rivers, and air. Freon, for example, is one chemical that can add to the holes in the ozone layer.

Tricycle Press
P.O. Box 7123
Berkeley, CA  94707
www.tenspeed.com

Design by Catherine Jacobes Design, San Francisco
Typeset in Folio and Zurich

Library of Congress Cataloging-in-Publication Data

Mitchell, Joyce Slayton.
  Crashed, smashed, and mashed : a trip to junkyard
heaven / Joyce Slayton Mitchell ; photographs by
Steven Borns.
      p. cm.
  ISBN 1-58246-034-5
  1.  Automobile graveyards—Juvenile literature. [1.
Automobile graveyards. 2. Junk.]  I. Borns, Steven, ill.
II. Title.
  TD795.4 .M58 2001
  629.2'028'6—dc21
                                                  00-010713

First printing, 2001
Printed in Singapore

1 2 3 4 5 6 - 05 04 03 02 01

*Check out these websites for more information
about junkyards and recycling:*
www.autorecyc.org
www.autobpa.com
www.u-r-g.com